Hebrews

13 STUDIES FOR INDIVIDUALS AND GROUPS

N. T. WRIGHT

with PATTY PELL

An imprint of InterVarsity Press
Downers Grove, Illinois

InterVarsity Press
P.O. Box 1400, Downers Grove, IL 60515-1426
World Wide Web: www.ivpress.com
E-mail: email@ivpress.com

This study guide is based on and includes excerpts adapted from Hebrews for Everyone, © 2003, 2004 Nicholas Thomas Wright. All Scripture quotations, unless otherwise indicated, are taken from the New Testament for Everyone. Copyright © 2001-2008 by Nicholas Thomas Wright. Used by permission of SPCK, London. All rights reserved.

InterVarsity Press® is the book-publishing division of InterVarsity Christian Fellowship/USA®, a movement of students and faculty active on campus at hundreds of universities, colleges and schools of nursing in the United States of America, and a member movement of the International Fellowship of Evangelical Students. For information about local and regional activities, write Public Relations Dept., InterVarsity Christian Fellowship/USA, 6400 Schroeder Rd., P.O. Box 7895, Madison, WI 53707-7895, or visit the IVCF website at <www.intervarsity.org>.

Design: Cindy Kiple
Cover image: Paul Knight/Trevillion Images

ISBN 978-0-8308-2195-2

Printed in the United States of America ∞

P   18   17   16   15   14   13   12   11   10   9   8   7

Y   25   24   23   22   21   20   19   18   17

CONTENTS

GETTING THE MOST
OUT OF HEBREWS

Half the fun of Christmas morning, especially for young children, is the exciting packages in glittering wrapping, with ribbons and bows, all telling you something about how wonderful the present itself will be. Many small children are so excited by the wrapping and the beautiful boxes that they almost ignore the present itself.

The writer of the letter of Hebrews is anxious that the people it is written to should not make that same mistake. The wrapping of the old covenant and its sacrificial system had come off the present; and the present was Jesus himself, God's own, unique son, sent to fulfill everything the law and the prophets had spoken of. They could move on from the earlier stages of God's purpose and gladly live out the new one which had dawned. Hebrews is written to urge its readers to not go back to their old ways.

We don't know who wrote the letter of Hebrews, but we do know it was written to Jewish Christians (who of course formed the nucleus of the earliest church). In the very last chapter, Hebrews 13, we have small indications of the situation of the writer and the readers. Verse 19, which sounds similar to what Paul says in Philemon 22, may indicate that the writer is in prison, though nothing elsewhere in the letter leads us to suspect that. Maybe he is simply engaged in difficult work which prevents him from coming to them at the moment.

The sudden mention of Timothy in 13:23, and of his being released, links this letter to Paul's world, but frustratingly doesn't help us get much further with identifying its writer or place of origin. The mention of those from Italy in 13:24 doesn't necessarily mean that the writer was in Italy at the time; it might easily indicate that there was a small community, wherever he was, who had come from Italy—consisting perhaps of those, like the people mentioned in Acts 18:2, who had been expelled from Rome by Claudius. Saying "Italy" instead of "Rome" may well be a note of caution, so as not to put Christians there in jeopardy should the letter fall into the wrong hands. (For more on this letter, also see my *Hebrews for Everyone,* published by SPCK and Westminster John Knox. This guide is based on that book and was prepared with the help of Patty Pell, for which I am grateful.)

This letter seems to be written not in the very earliest period of the church, but perhaps some time between A.D. 50 and A.D. 70, possibly even after that. For many Jewish Christians things were not easy. Lots of their family members and friends and neighbors had not accepted Jesus as the long-awaited Messiah, and they regarded them as dangerous, misguided and disloyal to all that God had said earlier on. All sorts of pressure would have been put on them to try and make them go back to where they had been before, to abandon this new-found movement with its strange claims and to take up again a position of living under God's law, the law given through Moses.

We know from chapter 10 (verses 32-34) that persecution was a problem for the recipients of this letter. And the writer seeks to further encourage his readers in chapter 11 with examples of those who held to their faith, often in the midst of very difficult circumstances.

Thus, Hebrews was written to show that you can't go back to an earlier stage of God's purposes, but must instead go forward, must press on eagerly from within the new stage to the one that is yet to come. The letter is a call to not play with the wrapping instead of with the brilliant present itself.

SUGGESTIONS FOR INDIVIDUAL STUDY

1. As you begin each study, pray that God will speak to you through his Word.

2. Read the introduction to the study and respond to the "Open" question that follows it. This is designed to help you get into the theme of the study.

3. Read and reread the Bible passage to be studied. Each study is designed to help you consider the meaning of the passage in its context. The commentary and questions in this guide are based on my own translation of each passage found in the companion volume to this guide in the For Everyone series on the New Testament (published by SPCK and Westminster John Knox).

4. Write your answers to the questions in the spaces provided or in a personal journal. Each study includes three types of questions: observation questions, which ask about the basic facts in the passage; interpretation questions, which delve into the meaning of the passage; and application questions, which help you discover the implications of the text for growing in Christ. Writing out your responses can bring clarity and deeper understanding of yourself and of God's Word.

5. Each session features selected comments from the For Everyone series. These notes provide further biblical and cultural background and contextual information. They are designed not to answer the questions for you but to help you along as you study the Bible for yourself. For even more reflections on each passage, you may wish to have on hand a copy of the companion volume from the For Everyone series as you work through this study guide.

6. Use the guidelines in the "Pray" section to focus on God, thanking him for what you have learned and praying about the applications that have come to mind.

SUGGESTIONS FOR GROUP MEMBERS

1. Come to the study prepared. Follow the suggestions for individual study mentioned above. You will find that careful preparation will greatly enrich your time spent in group discussion.

2. Be willing to participate in the discussion. The leader of your group will not be lecturing. Instead, she or he will be asking the questions found in this guide and encouraging the members of the group to discuss what they have learned.

3. Stick to the topic being discussed. These studies focus on a particular passage of Scripture. Only rarely should you refer to other portions of the Bible or outside sources. This allows for everyone to participate on equal ground and for in-depth study.

4. Be sensitive to the other members of the group. Listen attentively when they describe what they have learned. You may be surprised by their insights! Each question assumes a variety of answers. Many questions do not have "right" answers, particularly questions that aim at meaning or application. Instead the questions push us to explore the passage more thoroughly.

   When possible, link what you say to the comments of others. Also, be affirming whenever you can. This will encourage some of the more hesitant members of the group to participate.

5. Be careful not to dominate the discussion. We are sometimes so eager to express our thoughts that we leave too little opportunity for others to respond. By all means participate! But allow others to also.

6. Expect God to teach you through the passage being discussed and through the other members of the group. Pray that you will have an enjoyable and profitable time together, but also that as a result of the study you will find ways that you can take action individually and/ or as a group.

7. It will be helpful for groups to follow a few basic guidelines. These guidelines, which you may wish to adapt to your situation, should be read at the beginning of the first session.

   • Anything said in the group is considered confidential and will not be discussed outside the group unless specific permission is given to do so.

- We will provide time for each person present to talk if he or she feels comfortable doing so.

- We will talk about ourselves and our own situations, avoiding conversation about other people.

- We will listen attentively to each other.

- We will be very cautious about giving advice.

Additional suggestions for the group leader can be found at the back of the guide.

GOD'S ONE AND ONLY SON

Hebrews 1

The ancient world did not have printing presses such as we do in the modern world, but it had equivalents, particularly for making coins. The emperor would employ an engraver who carved the royal portrait, and suitable words or abbreviations, on a stamp, or die, made of hard metal. The engraver used the stamp to make a coin, so that the coin gave the exact impression, indeed expression, of what was on the stamp.

The writer of Hebrews begins the letter with this idea. It is as though the exact imprint of the Father's very nature and glory has been precisely reproduced in the soft metal of the Son's human nature.

OPEN

How do you see people in the surrounding culture trying to experience and expand their spirituality?

STUDY

1. *Read Hebrews 1.* This chapter is a grand and formal opening to this letter to the Hebrews.

What do we learn in particular about Jesus in verses 1-4?

2. How does the writer invite us in verses 1-4 to look at the whole sweep of biblical history and see it coming to a climax in Jesus?

3. In verse 5, two Old Testament passages are quoted: Psalm 2:7 and 2 Samuel 7:14. These two passages were frequently used by the early Christians when they were struggling to say what had to be said about Jesus. How do these quotes further explain who Jesus is?

4. The writer quotes from two psalms (97:7 and 104:4) in verses 6-7. How do these verses contrast Jesus and angels?

5. In verses 8-9, Psalm 45:6-7 is being quoted. The psalm addresses the king as if he can be called God, but the writer of Hebrews applies this psalm to Jesus, the Messiah. What will the reign of the Messiah be like according to this psalm?

6. When you think of the condition of the world today, where do you long to see the reign of Jesus?

7. Why might the writer of Hebrews have chosen to include the quotes from Psalm 102:25-27 in verses 10-12?

8. A third psalm is quoted in verse 13: Psalm 110. Once again, in verses 13-14 the writer contrasts Jesus with the angels, though in a different way. What is the role of the angels compared to that of the Messiah?

9. As mentioned in the introduction, many of the Jewish believers in the early church had family members who had not accepted that Jesus was the Messiah, and they regarded the Jewish believers as dangerously misguided and disloyal. Great pressure was exerted on the Jewish believers to turn back to the law, which according to Jewish tradition had been given to Moses by angels on Mount Sinai.

In what ways do verses 5-14 help establish Jesus' superiority over the law?

10. Not many readers today, perhaps, will be tempted to abandon Christianity in favor of some form of Judaism—though it is important for us to understand why that was such an obvious pressure in the early days. But many today, including many in the churches, seem dissatisfied with what they have, and are eager to expand their spiritual horizons (as they might see it) to include angels, saints and other interesting distractions.

What specific ways are you and your church or faith community tempted to expand your spiritual horizons?

11. The angels, the law and the prophets were all part of God's preparation, part of the brilliant and beautiful wrapping in which the ultimate present, God's gift of his own self in the person of the Son, would be contained. How can you pay closer attention to who Jesus is and to the role of worship and service to which he has called you, instead of playing with the "wrapping"?

PRAY

Spend time in worship giving praise to the Messiah. Focus on Jesus as the ultimate climax to all of history, and give specific prayers of thanks for the aspects of his reign.

2

JESUS AS THE
TRULY HUMAN BEING

Hebrews 2

Imagine being in a little motorboat, some way out from shore, needing to find your way along the coast to the right harbor. You need to keep the engine running and a firm hand on the tiller. If you don't, there is no guarantee that you will drift in the right direction, and every probability that you will drift in the wrong one—perhaps onto a rocky shore or out to the wild ocean.

Hebrews 2 is a warning many believers need. It is all too easy to suppose that we can take the pressure off and allow other people to do the praying, the thinking, the serious business; we'll go along for the ride, we'll stop putting so much effort into it, we'll go with the flow. The problem is that if we haven't got our own motor running and our own hand on the tiller, we may drift further and further away without realizing it.

OPEN

Describe a time when someone gave you a warning that you didn't pay much attention to. What happened?

STUDY

1. *Read Hebrews 2.* As mentioned before, according to Jewish tradition
    the law came to Moses through angels—and look what happens if
    people ignore *that*. Now: what will happen if they refuse to listen
    to something even more important and powerful? God may have to
    conclude that they really aren't interested in being rescued, in being
    saved from the sin and injustice which rages around them like an
    angry sea. That's why, in this passage and frequently later on, He-
    brews insists not just that Christians must stick with what they've
    got, rather than abandoning it, but also that they must pay *closer*
    attention, must go deeper into the truth and life which is theirs be-
    cause they belong to the Messiah.

    In what different ways, according to 2:1-4, was the message of salva-
    tion in Christ emphasized?

2. How does this compare and contrast with the message that came
    through angels?

3. What evidence is there in your life or in your Christian community
    that the message of Jesus is true and powerful?

4. In what ways does the writer speak about both the *future* role of
    Jesus in God's new creation and his *present* position in verses 5-9?

5. In a parliamentary democracy, voters in each area elect someone to *represent* them in the central councils of state. They can't all be there themselves so they find an appropriate way of appointing someone who is there *on their behalf*, carrying their hopes, fears, needs and aspirations, in his or her own person. Thus, because the representative is there and they are not, he or she also acts as their *substitute*, doing for them what, for various reasons, they can't do for themselves.

   How is Jesus being portrayed as the representative in verses 5-9?

6. What does it mean to you on a daily basis that Jesus Christ has already dealt with death on our behalf and is already ruling the world as its rightful Lord?

7. What different family images do you find in Hebrews 2:10-18?

8. This passage of Hebrews depicts Jesus as the kind of older brother who, without a trace of patronizing or looking down his nose at us, comes to find us where we are, out of sheer love and goodness of heart, and to help us out of the mess.

   How does the writer of Hebrews say in verses 10-18 that Jesus rescues humanity?

9. Another major theme from the entire letter of Hebrews is introduced in verses 17-18—Jesus as the high priest, a theme we'll see more of in the letter. In what ways does Jesus fulfill the role of high priest?

10. Looking at 2:10-18, in what ways is Jesus like a pioneer?

11. Which image from chapter 2 (such as representative, older brother, high priest, pioneer) connects with you the most and why?

12. How does this image help you to "keep your hand on the tiller" of your boat and continue to live in faith?

PRAY

Take some time to sit in silence and meditate on the image of Jesus in this passage that resonates with you. What does Jesus seem to be saying to you through this image?

NOTE ON HEBREWS 2:5-9

The phrase "son of man," which to a Jewish reader could simply mean "a typical human being," could also, to someone familiar with the book of

Daniel (7:13; 8:17) or the teaching of Jesus, mean "the Messiah"—highlighting the fact that the Messiah is now to be seen as the true, typical, authentic and representative human being. This is what Hebrews has in mind, as we can see from the last line of the quotation about God placing everything under his feet.

This passage also highlights how Jesus has already attained the status which God marked out for humans in general. Here we meet a point which we shall discover to be typical of the way Hebrews understands the Old Testament. Psalm 8, quoted in Hebrews 2:6-8, speaks of humankind in general as set in authority over the world, with "everything subject to him." But, says Hebrews, this clearly hasn't happened yet. Humans are not ruling the world in a way that brings God's order and justice to bear on the whole of creation. Everything is still in a state of semi-chaos. How then can this psalm be taken seriously?

The answer is that it *has* happened—in the case of Jesus. He is the representative of the human race. He has gone ahead of the rest of us into God's future, the future in which order and justice—saving order, healing justice—will come into the world.

Hold On Tight!

Hebrews 3

Enthusiastic beginnings, grumbling when things got tough, and then provision of enough to go on with describes more or less the wanderings of the children of Israel in the wilderness after they had come out of Egypt.

At this point in Hebrews there is something of the same narrative sequence. There has been discussion of Moses and the giving of the law, and now the writer talks about the wilderness wanderings, the forty years they all spent in the desert before, finally, they were allowed to enter the land they had been promised. During that time they went through what the writer of Psalm 95 calls "the great bitterness," the time when the people faced the test of whether or not they were going to trust God to provide for them, and they in turn put God to the test by demanding signs of his presence and care. Some even wanted to go back to Egypt and slavery thinking they'd at least be fed there.

The author of Hebrews wants to challenge readers to remember that previous generation who walked through the wilderness so they don't make the same mistakes.

OPEN

Give an example of when you were really passionate about something but over time that passion faded away. Why did the passion fade?

STUDY

1. *Read Hebrews 3.* What does the writer mean when he says in verse 1 that his readers share the call from heaven?

2. How does the writer compare and contrast Moses and Jesus in the first six verses of chapter 3?

3. Most first-century Jews, when presented with the idea of "God's house," would think at once of the temple. But Hebrews and Paul, and also some other radical Jewish groups of the period, thought of the true "house" not as a building of bricks and mortar but as a community of people. The people who make up this house are described in verse 6 as a bold, confident family. They are people who, as verse 1 says, are willing to confess their belief in Jesus.

Why are we sometimes unwilling to state this belief to others?

4. The writer of Hebrews uses Psalm 95, which chronicles the desert wanderings, to make his point in verses 7-11. How is the experience of the Israelites wandering in the desert similar to and different from the position the early Christians were in?

5. What is the main challenge the writer of Hebrews is making to the early believers in verses 12-13?

6. Many of the people in the wilderness stopped believing that God was really with them, really leading them. They simply stopped believing in God's promises and instead believed a lie. Hebrews is concerned with something similar—whether or not Jewish Christians continue to follow and trust Jesus, or waiver and drift back to the law.

   What old ways are you tempted to return to instead of continuing to trust God in Christ?

7. In what ways can we guard against drifting away and hardening our hearts?

8. What does it mean to share the life of Christ, the Messiah (v. 14), in the context of this chapter?

9. The writer returns to the desert wanderings with three probing questions in verses 16, 17 and 18. What point is the writer trying to make with these questions?

10. Psalm 95:7-8 (quoted in Hebrews 3:7-8 and repeated in 3:15) emphasizes that people face a choice. The challenge becomes more urgent with the word *today*. Along with the other early Christians, the writer believed passionately that God had acted once for all in Jesus the Messiah, and that as a result the new day had dawned for which Israel had been waiting. They had been living in "tomorrow mode" for long enough. Now it was "today mode," the moment when suddenly it was all happening. If they would remember that, they would stay on track.

How can a focus on the fact that Jesus is at work right now in our world, bringing God's kingdom reign to earth, help us live more faithfully as followers of Jesus?

11. The writer of the Hebrews thinks it could be all too easy to be spiritually complacent. "We're not like Gentiles." "We've got the law from Moses." "We are from the lineage of Abraham." But the author of Hebrews wants us to note that it was in fact the people of Israel

who complained, who rebelled and who were punished by God as a result. So we ought not to think we are above these sorts of problems or attitudes. We too could fall. This warning, the writer is insisting, isn't for the person standing next to you. It's for you. Yes, you.

Why might we be tempted to think we couldn't fall or drift away from Christ?

12. How can we fight spiritual complacency?

PRAY

Pray about how you are tempted to drift back to old ways of relying on other things or people besides Jesus. Ask God to keep you from complacency and to help you keep a firm, tight grip on him.

GETTING THROUGH TO THE SABBATH REST

Hebrews 4:1-13

In biblical theology there is a principle of "one day in seven," or possibly "one year in seven," or some variation on these, which is built into creation from the beginning. By the time of Jesus, the parts of the Mosaic law which dealt with sabbath observance had become such a tightly drawn legal system that people were forgetting their purpose, which was to help people by giving them rest, not to add burdens to them by forbidding things like healing. Jesus had to break through all that, as we see in the Gospels, but nowhere does the New Testament deny that the principle set out in Genesis 1 remains important: a day of rest once a week, corresponding to God's day of rest at the end of creation. In Hebrews chapter 4 the idea of God's rest on the seventh day of creation comes into its own in a different way.

OPEN

Describe what a perfectly restful day would be like for you.

STUDY

1. *Read Hebrews 4:1-13.* The writer has already used Psalm 95 to talk about the "rest" which the Israelites had been promised once they reached their destination (see Hebrews 3:15). In Hebrews 4:3, the author quotes Psalm 95 again, alongside examples of other kinds of rest.

   What two other examples or types of rest are described in 4:1-10?

2. How are the three "rests" different from one another?

3. The writer of Hebrews speaks about "entering the rest" five times in verses 1-13. What prevents someone from entering the "rest"?

4. What different things can cause us to trip and fall into unbelief?

5. Verse 10 says that anyone who enters the future rest will take a rest from all their works. What kind of works does the writer have in mind?

6. All of us face the challenge to trust God rather than to trust the way we feel or the things we see in front of us. How can we keep before our eyes the promise of God's eventual, and eternal, "rest"?

7. At the time Hebrews was written, the author may not have known about other books and letters that are in our New Testament—indeed some may not even have been written at this point. Was the author then referring just to the Old Testament when he mentions "God's word" in 4:12, or something more? Explain.

8. What does God's word do as seen in verses 11-13?

9. How does this help stem the steady erosion of belief that results in unbelief?

10. What obstacles keep you from spending time prayerfully and thoughtfully with Scripture and with Jesus, the written and living Word of God, who can touch you gently and powerfully?

If we open ourselves, day by day and week by week, to the message of Scripture, its grand sweep and its small details, and allow the faithful preaching of Jesus and his achievement to enter our consciousness and soak down into our imagination and heart, then the admittedly uncomfortable work of God's word will be happening on a regular basis, showing us (as we say) where we really are, what's going on deep inside.

11. While God's word is essential to our spiritual growth and for us to know what's going on deep inside, what else is needed and helpful in our lives for this?

12. What can you do specifically this week to allow the word of God to cleanse and heal you as it is described in verses 11-13?

PRAY

Take a few minutes to read through Psalm 95. Use the words of the psalm to direct you to Jesus and guide your prayer time.

NOTE ON HEBREWS 4:12

The way the New Testament writers use the phrase "God's word" suggests that they meant more (not less) than the Old Testament. They also meant the message which Jesus announced—that God's kingdom was coming to birth in and through his work—and then the message *about* Jesus and what he'd done, essentially the same message but from a new perspective. However, since the point of what Jesus had done was precisely that it fulfilled the prophecies of the Old Testament, which is after all what this letter is mostly about, we can put the two together quite easily. "God's word" seems to mean "the ancient scriptures, and the message about how they all came true in Jesus."

5

THE SON BECOMES
THE PRIEST

Hebrews 4:14–5:14

There was a son who inherited a business from his father. It sounds like a rather grand thing—the son comes in to sit in a splendid office and enjoy the lifestyle of business lunches, golf outings, foreign trips and all the rest—but it wasn't a bit like that. The father made sure that the son learned the business from the ground up. He had to work in the workshops along with the hardened mechanics. He had to visit the suppliers to see where the raw materials came from, and find out for himself how hard it was to get them at the right price. He had to go out as a salesman into the suspicious world that wasn't convinced it wanted the product. And he had to share the work of the financial department as they spent day after day crunching the complicated numbers. Only when he had thoroughly understood every aspect of how the business worked was he even given an office of his own.

Now he would have to learn both how to lead and how to manage a workforce as well as how to represent the business in the wider world. He had to learn what it meant to be the son of his father. This story goes some way toward explaining some of the oddest phrases in the whole letter of Hebrews, which are found in chapter 5.

OPEN

Talk about a difficult lesson you've learned and how you learned it. How did this experience give you compassion for others who are in similar situations?

STUDY

1. *Read Hebrews 4:14–5:14.* How does Jesus fulfill the role of a high priest as explained in verses 4:14–5:10?

Don't make the mistake that some Christians have made of imagining that Jesus, having become human in the incarnation, stopped being human after his death. One of the central beliefs of the early Christians, not least in this letter and those of Paul, is that Jesus remains fully and gloriously human, and that it is as a human being that he rules the world. When he represents us before the Father, he isn't looking down on us from a great height and being patronizing about those poor creatures down there who can't really do much for themselves. He can truly sympathize. He has been here. He knows exactly what it's like.

2. How do these same verses say that Jesus surpassed the function of the high priest of Israel?

3. Once Jesus was resurrected he did not simply go to a convenient resting place in some spiritual sphere where he could remain, satisfied with having accomplished his earthly work. According to verses 4:14, where is Jesus now and what is he presently doing?

4. How does it affect you knowing that Jesus can sympathize with your weaknesses (4:15)?

5. In light of this, what does it look like for believers to approach the throne of grace with confidence (4:16)?

6. There is evidence that Jews may have criticized the early Christian movement, and Jesus himself, for apparently snatching at a position which belonged, uniquely and forever, to the temple in Jerusalem. How does Hebrews 5:4-6 address this concern?

We will hear more about Melchizedek in Hebrews 6–7. For the moment we can say that he meets Abraham briefly in Genesis 14:18-20. He was a priest of the Most High God, but obviously not of Aaron's priesthood, since Aaron (along with Moses) lived hundreds of years later.

7. What scenes from Jesus' life are called to mind by 5:7-8?

8. How does this help explain what it meant for Jesus to learn to be a son?

9. Verses 11-14 of chapter 5 are a remarkable rebuke that bursts upon us, and must have burst upon its first hearers, like a sudden cold shower. The writer clearly wants to wake the readers up with a double challenge. Of what is the writer accusing the believers?

10. What is the nature of "maturity" that the writer has in mind?

11. When is it hard for you to distinguish between behavior that is right and behavior that isn't?

12. How can we grow in our ability to distinguish the two?

The word for *justice* is a tricky one wherever we meet it in the New Testament; it's often translated "righteousness," but that gives people the impression that it's all about behaving yourself in a rather self-consciously religious fashion, which certainly isn't what He-brews (or the other early Christians) had in mind. *Justice* doesn't quite catch the full flavor, either, but at least it makes the point that the purposes of God in the gospel are focused on God's longing to put the world right, and to put people right as part of that work. The writer here longs for people to understand the entire message of God's healing, restoring, saving justice. He wants them to be able to handle this message in relation to their own lives, their communities and the wider world.

PRAY

Practice praying with confidence as you approach the throne of grace. Spend a few minutes praying and meditating on the truth that Jesus sympathizes with you.

NOTE ON HEBREWS 5:8-9

Although Jesus was God's Son, he learned the nature of obedience through what he suffered. One might have thought (the writer seems to be saying) that being God's Son would simply be a matter of sharing God's rule of the world, living in glory and bliss. Not so. The God who is the Father of Jesus is the God who made the world in the first place, and he remains deeply committed to his creation, even though it has become wayward and corrupt. Jesus must learn what it means to be his Father's obedient Son; and that will mean suffering, not because God is a sadist who simply wants to see his dear Son having a rough time of it, but because the world which God made and loves is a dark and wicked place and the Son must suffer its sorrow and pain in order to rescue it.

When it says that Jesus was made complete and perfect, it doesn't mean that he was imperfect before in the sense of being sinful. Rather he needed to attain the full stature of sonship through experiencing the pain and grief of the Father himself over his world gone wrong. He be-came truly and fully what in his nature he already was.

6

KEEP UP THE GOOD WORK

Hebrews 6

Most of us have started projects and have gotten bogged down. Often we discover that there are several distinct phases to the process: the initial burst of enthusiasm and the excitement of something quite new, the gradual seeping away of energy as we reach the hard grind of carrying on, and then the days, and perhaps the weeks and even years, when we get out of bed without enthusiasm, without desire to work on the project, wishing we could have some other novelty to excite us but realizing that there is a goal ahead which will make it all worthwhile if only we can put one foot in front of another until we get there.

Living as a Christian is often like that, and the writer of Hebrews knows that his readers may be in just that situation.

OPEN

What projects have you gotten bogged down with and why?

STUDY

1. *Read Hebrews 6.* What is meant by each of the basic teachings of the Christian faith found in verses 1-2?

2. Why are these things we shouldn't have to go back over again once we've begun our Christian life?

3. Sometimes, of course, Christians never learned these things properly in the first place. What steps could you or your fellowship take to make sure people have a good grasp of why people are baptized, what precisely the resurrection is and why we should believe it, what "dead works" are and why we should repent of them?

4. Verses 4-5 offer a lavish description of what happens when you become a Christian. Expand on what is meant by each phrase.

5. The writer is saying that he is *not* going to go back over all the same ground again. Rather, he wants to go deeper, to teach them more developed and wide-ranging truths. How does the metaphor about the land in verses 7-8 illustrate his reasons for this?

6. Verse 6 raises an interesting question, which the writer doesn't pursue here: is it possible first to become a genuine Christian and then to lose everything after all? To this question Paul, in Romans 5–8, gives the emphatic answer "No!" In Hebrews the writer quickly goes on to say that he doesn't think his readers come into the category he's describing (6:9), but he chooses not to unpack this wider theological question.

The normal way of holding what he says together with what Paul says is that the people described in verses 4 and 5 are those who have become church members, and have felt the power of the gospel and the life that results from it through sharing the common life of Christian fellowship but who have never really made it their own, deep down inside.

The question the writer poses for all of us is: What might entice us or some within our Christian fellowship to turn our backs on the faith and join in the general tendency to sneer at the gospel and the church?

7. In 6:10-12 the writer encourages his readers to continue strong in their active love for others. How would you compare your level of energy and enthusiasm for acts of love and service now, compared to when you first became a Christian? Explain.

8. What specific act of love or service could you engage in this week?

9. In Hebrews 6:1 the author talks about the foundation in the Christian life of repentance from dead works and of faith toward God. Now in 6:9-12 he encourages energetic participation in that life and warns against laziness. How can we balance the truths of God's faithfulness and our own human effort in daily life as believers?

10. The "two unchangeable things" mentioned in 6:18 are God's promise to Abraham and the oath he swore by himself that he would keep the promise (6:13-14, 17). God can't lie in either of them. This is why the promise can and must be regarded as firm and secure; and this, in turn, explains what lies underneath the exhortations in the previous passage to hold on to hope and to persevere in faith.

The rest of the chapter explores the life of Abraham, the classic biblical example of faithful patience. How does the life of Abraham in verses 13-20 encourage the believers?

11. "Behind the curtain" (6:19) refers to the great moment, once a year, when the high priest goes into the temple, behind the last curtain, into the innermost sanctuary of the temple, into the holy of holies. There, on what Jews believed was the holiest spot on earth, the high priest would make atonement for the people. Jesus, through his death, resurrection and ascension, went into the very presence of the loving Father, and we are attached to him as though by a great cable. He is there, in the very presence of God, like an anchor. As long as we don't let go of the cable, we are anchored to the presence of God.

How is Jesus in this way our anchor in the storms of life?

12. Christian faith isn't optimism, a vague sense that things will proba-
    bly turn out right. Christian faith is trusting—and going on trusting
    through thick and thin—in the God who made unbreakable prom-
    ises and will certainly keep them.

    Where in your life do you need to keep on trusting God's promises?

PRAY

Pray in silence for a few moments and meditate on God's promises. Ask
God to speak his promises to you and then listen for his voice.

NOTE ON HEBREWS 6:9-12

Ever since the Reformation in the sixteenth century, many Christians
have been taught, quite rightly, that nothing we can do can earn God's
favor. Grace remains grace; God loves us because he loves us, not because we manage to do a few things to impress him, or to notch up a few
points on some heavenly scorecard. But at the same time the whole New
Testament insists that what Christians *do* matters a great deal.

Yes, there are undoubtedly times when, like the children of Israel
beside the Red Sea, we need the message that says, "The Lord will fight
for you; all you need to do is to be still" (Exodus 14:14). But these are the
exceptional moments, the particular situations, often in times of emer-
gency, when there is nothing we can or should do, and we must trust
that God will do it all. But the normal Christian life is one of energy,
enthusiasm, faithful effort and patient hard work.

When Paul tells the Philippians to "work out their own salvation with
fear and trembling," he at once adds, "because God is at work in you"
(Philippians 2:12-13). The energy to do all that we are called to do comes
itself from God working within us in the power of the Holy Spirit.

7

THE PERMANENT
PRIESTHOOD OF JESUS
Hebrews 7

Sometimes when you are working on a particular subject or studying a topic, you will come across something that you do not understand or know. Maybe it is a name or a place. So, you might go to the relevant dictionary or reference materials and look it up. Suddenly, from a small question about a single person or topic, a whole new area of thought, history or culture opens up in front of you. You can get a view of the wide sweep of the ancient world, and when you come back to the original task, you carry with you all the information about that one person or topic. What started off as a small puzzle in the middle of your work has turned into a lighthouse sending rays of light flashing over the rest of the subject.

That is the effect that Hebrews wants to create with the discussion of Melchizedek in chapter 7. This passage takes us into what seems at first sight a technical, almost bizarre discussion of a short reference in Genesis, but leads us to a place where the rays of light are flashing over the entire topic.

OPEN

Talk about a time when you discovered a "better" way to do something. Perhaps it was a new way to build something, a better way to organize or a more compassionate approach to a problem. How did you feel about this discovery?

STUDY

1. *Read Hebrews 7.* The writer of Hebrews has quoted Psalm 110:4, tantalizingly, three times already (5:6, 10 and 6:20). He, like many early Christians, has realized that Jesus has been appointed by God to a position at his right hand, waiting for his kingdom to be complete (Psalm 110:1). According to the psalm, the Messiah, the one to whom all things are put into subjection, is appointed by God as a priest forever, according to the order of Melchizedek. To find out what the psalmist meant, the writer of Hebrews, in 7:1-10, reviews some key points from Genesis 14, the only other passage in the whole Bible where Melchizedek is mentioned.

   What do we learn about Melchizedek from Hebrews 7:1-10?

2. Levi, one of the twelve sons of Jacob and a great-grandson of Abraham, founded the priestly tribe of Israel. How does 7:4-10 make the case that Melchizedek's priesthood is superior to Levi's?

Some people have thought that the writer of Hebrews, finding in the text no mention of Melchizedek's parents or ancestors (or his birth or death), has concluded that Melchizedek didn't have any. This is unnecessary and unlikely. The point is that no mention is made of where he got his priesthood—in particular, there is no mention that he inherited it through his family as priests of Levi did. It is as though, the writer says, Melchizedek is just there—a permanent fixture.

3. How are Melchizedek and Jesus similar as seen in these verses?

4. A first-century Jew would have found it striking that one person could be both king and priest since there was a clear division between those two roles in the history of Israel. Discovering more about Melchizedek, and so discovering what Psalm 110 meant when talking of the Messiah as a priest as well as a king, is a way to increase and deepen our sense of trust and assurance as we lean the full weight of our future hope on Jesus and on him alone.

In what different ways or areas of your life do you gain assurance knowing that Jesus is king but is also our high priest?

5. What further contrasts are outlined in verses 11-19 between Jesus' priesthood and the priesthood of Levi and his descendant Aaron?

6. The word often translated as "perfection" in 7:11 and 19 can also
   be translated as "completeness." It is when everything has been put
   into place for the final great purpose to be achieved. What is this
   great purpose (verses 11-19)?

7. The word *better* (or at least the Greek word which it here translates)
   occurs more times in Hebrews than in the whole of the rest of the
   New Testament put together. The writer is constantly contrasting—
   not something bad with something good, but something good with
   something better. He is not saying that the ancient Israelite system
   was a bad thing, with its temple, its law and its priesthood of Levi.
   What he is saying is that something new has arrived in and through
   Jesus which is *even better* than what went before.

   What was the purpose of the old religious system?

8. What examples have you seen of God, through the new system in
   Jesus, bringing this world to completion?

9. In chapters 4 and 5, we noted one half of the meaning of Jesus' high
   priesthood. He is a truly human being, tempted in every respect just
   as we are. Now, in verses 20-28, we discover the other half of the
   picture.

What does Jesus' superiority to other priests mean for our salvation?

10. Some Christians face the danger of forgetting just how central and vital Jesus himself was and is to every aspect of Christian faith. How do we tend to forget the centrality of Jesus?

11. This chapter of Hebrews should bring us to a place of gratitude and hope after we truly grasp the work of Jesus in his death and resurrection. In what ways can you express your gratitude to Jesus this week?

PRAY

Use short expressions of praise and gratitude for all that Jesus is and for all that he has accomplished for the world and for you individually.

The Promise of
a New Covenant

Hebrews 8

Years ago there was a toy which simulated the game of football. It was a table-top version that was played with plastic figures an inch or two high. It was played by flicking the figures with a finger, so that they would hit the ball and try to get it into the opponent's goal in the usual way. You could become quite good at the game, particularly if you were small and have active little fingers. But if you ever saw an actual football match you would never mistake the table-top variety for the real thing.

Supposing, however, that the game was given to a family who had not only never seen a real football match but who didn't know that such a thing existed. They might imagine that table-top football was the reality; this was all there was. They wouldn't know that it was a copy of the real thing, and gained most of its meaning, and its appeal for most people, because it was reminding them of the true, grown-up version.

Something like this, only more so, lies at the heart of the contrast Hebrews now draws in chapter 8 and will go on drawing.

OPEN

Why are people sometimes satisfied with a copy or a lower-quality product rather than the real thing?

STUDY

1. *Read Hebrews 8.* How does the writer describe the present and continuing role of Jesus in verses 1-6?

2. What do you think and feel in response to this?

3. In the Bible heaven is not simply a "spiritual," in the sense of nonphysical, dimension. It is God's space, God's realm, which interlocks with our realm in all sorts of ways. The Israelites believed that the temple in Jerusalem was the place above all where heaven and earth met, quite literally. When you went into the temple, especially when you went into the holy of holies in the middle of it, you were actually going into heaven itself.

What evidence does the writer of Hebrews provide that the tabernacle was a copy of the real thing (Hebrews 8:5 and Exodus 25:40)?

4. This passage draws together for the last time the contrast between Jesus and the priesthood before him. How do verses 1-6 outline this final contrast?

5. The readers of Hebrews are encouraged not to cling to the copy. This must have presented a particular challenge to those Jewish Christians who all their lives had looked to the Jerusalem temple as the focus of devotion, the place of pilgrimage, the very house of God, and to the priests who served there.

   How do you see people today choosing to focus on a "copy" instead of on the reality of Jesus?

6. In verses 7-13, we are faced with the longest single biblical quotation so far in a letter which has more than its fair share. In what particular ways does the writer use this text from Jeremiah 31:31-34 to continue the theme of something "better"?

7. What reasons do these verses give for the necessity of a new covenant?

8. The promises God made to Abraham and his family, and the require-

ments that were laid on them as a result, came to be seen in terms either of the agreement that a king would make with a subject people, or sometimes of the marriage bond between husband and wife. One regular way of describing this relationship was "covenant," which can thus include both promises and law. The original covenant with Abraham was renewed with Moses at Mount Sinai with the giving of the Law. Jeremiah 31 promised that after the punishment of exile God would make a new covenant with his people, forgiving them and binding them to him more intimately.

Do you find that external constraints (like the law) or internal changes (like of mind and heart) better help you do what's right? Why?

9. What does verse 12 highlight about the new covenant?

10. What does it mean to you that God forgets your sins?

11. How would using the text from Jeremiah have strengthened the writer's argument for the importance of holding on to Jesus instead of going back to the apparent safety of Judaism?

12. How does it help you want to hold on to Jesus?

PRAY

Read several times the passage from Jeremiah 31 used in this chapter of Hebrews. Use the text as a guide for your prayers.

THE SACRIFICE OF
THE MESSIAH

Hebrews 9

When a large city is in the midst of a complicated construction project, alternative arrangements have to be made in order to allow the daily traffic to get through while the project is in process. Ordinary life has to go on and people still have to get to work. So, in addition to the eventual plan—the great design in the mind of the planners and somewhere no doubt in a model under a glass case in City Hall—there have to exist all sorts of preparatory and intermediate plans. While the work is going on, the city needs to build extra temporary roads going this way and that, which they will then demolish when the final stage is complete. No doubt this work, too, subdivides into several stages.

The main point to which Hebrews now comes, in one sense, is that God has all along had a master plan for how the world would be put right. Yet, for reasons that people may only be dimly aware of, this cannot be done all at once. Temporary arrangements have to be made to keep things flowing, to regulate ongoing human life, until the appointed time.

OPEN

Why do we sometimes favor the old over the new?

STUDY

1. *Read Hebrews 9:1-14.* Describe the structures and functions of the tabernacle that the writer recounts in verses 1-10.

2. Having brought up the new covenant of Jeremiah 31 in the last chapter, the writer of Hebrews is now reminding his readers of some key aspects of the old covenant. How does the double structure of the tabernacle, which was reflected in the temple in Jerusalem, serve as a picture or parable of the two "ages," the two periods of time, within the long purposes of God?

3. What do we learn about the sacrificial system from verses 11-14?

4. In what ways is the new covenant "better" or more superior to the former things in verses 11-14?

5. The God whom Israel has always worshiped but whose saving plan
   was still in the preliminary stage had revealed once and for all
   through Jesus' death and resurrection the way into his presence, the
   way by which his people could serve him gladly and joyfully without the slightest shadow or stain on their consciences (9:14). Many
   Christian people, still today, forget that they are called to that kind
   of joyful service, free from any motivation caused by guilt or fear.

   Why do you suppose that such a liberating and healing message
   would be so hard to believe and remember?

6. *Read Hebrews 9:15-28.* In what ways, according to the writer of Hebrews,
   does the way a will works help us understand how a covenant works?

7. The idea of no pardon without bloodshed can seem primitive or barbaric. Yet our modern society tolerates, even fosters, so many things
   that previous generations, and other civilizations today, would consider barbaric.

   The point of sacrifice within the Old Testament system was a com-
   bination of at least three things: (1) humans offering to God something which represented their own true selves, (2) the outpouring of
   life to signify dealing with sin, and (3) the effects of both of these in
   the cleansing or purifying of the worshiper. Now we go a stage further, even more mysteriously, into the heart of the second of these.
   Somehow, it seems, the blood of the sacrificial animals was point-
   ing forward to a deeper truth still: that at the heart of the sacrificial
   system there lies the self-giving love of God himself.

How does Jesus' sacrifice reveal God's love to us?

8. Continuing his theme of what is now "better," what more does the writer of Hebrews have to say in verses 23-28 about why Jesus' sacrifice is superior to those of the old covenant?

The writer of Hebrews explains that the heavenly sanctuary, like the earthly one, needed purifying, albeit in a superior fashion. This is bound to seem puzzling at first glance. Why should the heavenly sanctuary need to be purified? What could have been wrong with it? The answer, it seems, is that there wasn't anything wrong with the heavenly sanctuary itself, but that it needed to be made ready for the arrival of people with whom there had been a very great deal wrong—namely, sinful human beings. We can't come into the presence of a holy God that way, but we were nonetheless promised that somehow we would. Jesus, then, purifies the heavenly sanctuary itself so that when other human beings are welcomed into it they will find, as the Israelites found in the earthly sanctuary, that everything there too bears the mark of God's self-giving love.

9. The word in 9:26 that is translated as the "end" or "close" of the ages literally refers to something which joins on to something else, and so makes one or both of them complete. How do verses 26-28 tell us Christ's work is ultimately fulfilled?

10. If you thought you needed to marry your spouse every year, every month or every week in order to be married, it would mean you

hadn't really understood what the wedding ceremony was about in the first place. What does it tell us about Christ's sacrifice that it was something that only happened once for all?

11. What difference does this hope we have in Christ make to you now?

12. How does the complete sacrifice of Jesus strengthen your faith?

PRAY

Look back over this chapter and ponder what Christ has done for us. Let this guide your praise, worship and thanksgiving.

NOTE ON HEBREWS 9:24

Verse 24 speaks, literally, of Jesus appearing "before God's face." This was a powerful idea in Jewish tradition: seeing God's face was such a devastatingly awesome experience that even the angels which flanked God's presence had to veil their faces (Isaiah 6:2). Now Jesus has gone in to see the Father's face, and has done so on our behalf, against the day when we will share that glorious vision and do so unafraid, because of the blood which has purified us through and through.

COME TO WORSHIP

Hebrews 10

The shopping was all done, and all the food and drink had been brought back into the house. All the telephone calls had been made. The house was cleaned, straightened and decorated. The food was prepared. Then, at last, the people began to arrive. Friends, neighbors and family all turned up. It was a party!

Hebrews has now, if it can be put this way, done the shopping, made the telephone calls and cleaned the house. At last the invitation goes out: come to the party! Chapter 10 is the invitation to a party that the writer of Hebrews has been preparing. The writer has been collecting key passages from Scripture, calling up ideas and images both familiar and unfamiliar, shaping and polishing the exposition. It leads to chapter 10: come to worship!

OPEN

Are you ever reluctant to join others in worship? Why or why not?

STUDY

1. *Read Hebrews 10:1-18.* The problem with the sacrifices and offerings of the old covenant, says Hebrews, wasn't that they were physical, "earthly" in that sense. After all, Jesus' own sacrifice was just as earthly and physical as the animal sacrifices in the temple. What was the problem instead (vv. 1-4)?

2. How does the use of Psalm 40 in verses 5-10 point to something new and better?

3. For much of the world, and for much of history, the act of sitting down (v. 12) meant that you had finished your work. Most people stood to work and sat down to rest. That is the contrast being made between the work of the priests in the old covenant who stood to make sacrifices in the temple and the work of Jesus in the new covenant who sat down at the right hand of God (vv. 11-18).

   How is the truth that Jesus has fully completed the purposes of God a comfort to the believers Hebrews is addressing?

   We have a sense, here in chapter 10, of several strands of thought in the letter as a whole being drawn together and fitting into the eventual big picture the writer has all along been holding in his mind. The picture of Jesus as the Messiah, the truly human being, the great high priest after the order of Melchizedek, the one who has offered the perfect sacrifice through which the sin-forgiving new covenant has been established at last—all these belong together. The argument of the letter is about Jesus at every point. The result of discovering, with the help of the Old Testament, what Jesus has achieved is to realize that he has fulfilled God's purposes as set out in scripture, so that the only wise place to be is with him, rather than with those who cling to the signposts instead of the reality.

4. *Read Hebrews 10:19-39.* What, as seen in 10:22-23, should characterize us as we draw near to God in worship?

5. How are we dependent on God and his work for each of these?

6. What can we gain from joining others in worship (vv. 24-25)?

The danger of people thinking they could be Christians all by themselves was, it seems, present in the early church just as today. This may not have been due to people failing to realize what a corporate thing Christianity was and is, nor because they were lazy or didn't like the other Christians in their locality. Rather it could very well be that when there is a threat of persecution (see 10:32-34), it's much easier to escape notice if you avoid meeting together with other worshipers. Much safer just not to turn up. There's no place for that, declares Hebrews.

7. Which part of Hebrews 10:19-25 is most difficult for you to embrace in your own life and why?

8. We find some rather severe warnings in 10:26-31. Put into your own words the kind of person the author is referring to when he talks about those who "sin deliberately and knowingly" (v. 26) and "trample the son of God underfoot" (v. 29)?

9. Many of us are so unused to thinking of God's judgment at all that we bend over backwards to downplay warnings like this one. What difference would it make in our thinking about God and how he relates to humans if God didn't judge people who have systematically ordered their lives so as to become an embodiment of injustice and malice?

10. In 10:26-39 we get the clearest indication of the situation of the believers to whom this letter is addressed and the persecution they faced. Hebrews 10:26-31 is a warning about those who have come close to Christian faith, perhaps sharing in the life of Christian worship, and then turn around and publicly deny it all.

   Persecution or other troubles have tempted some, and can tempt us, to declare that Christ and the whole Christian life are worthless. What can help us resist such temptation?

11. What kinds of difficulties were the original readers of Hebrews facing (vv. 32-39)?

12. How is Habakkuk 2:3-4 (quoted in Hebrews 10:37-38) used to help the believers face their circumstances?

13. How do these words help you?

PRAY

The writer of Hebrews calls the believers to come and worship in complete assurance of faith. Spend several minutes worshiping God. Use Psalm 40 or some worship music to help you focus on praise and thanksgiving.

NOTE ON HEBREWS 10:1

Many readers have wondered if perhaps the writer is using ideas that had been made famous by the philosopher Plato. In particular, the idea of something being a "shadow" rather than a "real form" sounds like his well-known picture of the Cave, in which people who haven't yet been enlightened think they're looking at reality but are in fact only looking at shadows cast by objects that remain out of sight.

This appearance, though, is superficial. The contrast the writer is making is not, like Plato, the contrast between physical objects and nonphysical ideas, or "forms." As verse 1 insists, it is the contrast between the *present* and the *future* realities. Jesus, who has gone ahead of us into God's future reality, will reappear when that future reality bursts into the present for the whole world.

NOTE ON HEBREWS 10:26-31

The question of who precisely such warnings are aimed at is one which bothered the early church from the second and third century onward, and ought still to concern us today. Some saw it as referring to anyone who, at any point after baptism, committed any serious sin. That's why, in the third and fourth centuries in particular, many prominent church attenders put off baptism until the last possible moment—either before death, or, if they were called to ministry, before ordination! They were frightened lest, by subsequent sinning of whatever kind, they might forfeit their entire salvation. Others read it more in light of what happened when persecution arouse. Such passages as this, it was thought, applied principally to people who, under threat of physical violence or death, were prepared to blaspheme against Jesus and revile him.

Many in our day tend to react in the opposite way. We don't want to imagine God being angry with anyone. We are probably as greatly deceived as were those in earlier centuries who treated these passages as a warning not so much against sinning as against baptism.

It is absolutely basic to both Judaism and Christianity that there will come a time when the living God will bring his just and wise rule to bear fully and finally on the world. On that day those who willfully stand out against his rule, live a life which scorns the standards which emerge in creation itself and in God's good intention for it, and spurn all attempts at reformation or renewal, will face a punishment of destruction. We who have got as far at least as reading Hebrews, and trying to see what it might mean for us, should be all the more eager that there will never come a time when we might turn our backs wholesale on God in this way.

What Faith Really Means

Hebrews 11

Our little group of climbers walked through the mist not realizing that anyone else was there. We kept moving, knowing that we would face some difficult climbing, including a rocky crag, later on. When we reached a small plateau, the sky cleared and we noticed that there was another large group of climbers ahead of us. They must have started several hours earlier and appeared to have negotiated the crag successfully. I took out a set of binoculars to see the group ahead of us a little more clearly. There was a sparkle of light from where the climbers were. Sure enough: ice axes. Now we knew just what we would be facing and just what was needed to cope with it—and that it was possible to make it.

Hebrews has now reached a plateau from which there is an excellent view of those who have gone on before. Looking at them, the readers can discover for themselves what is up ahead, what they will need to cope with it, and the fact that when they get there themselves there will be a great welcome.

OPEN

Who are your spiritual heroes, strong believers who have faced difficult things faithfully? What about them is so encouraging to you?

STUDY

1. *Read Hebrews 11:1-22.* Explain how faith and hope are linked, as described in Hebrews 11:1?

2. What do we learn about faith through Abel and Enoch in 11:4-6?

3. Hebrews wants its readers to learn that faith is not a general religious attitude to life. It is not simply believing difficult or impossible things for the sake of it, as though simple credulity was itself a virtue. So what do we learn about what faith really is from Noah, Abraham and Sarah in 11:7-12?

4. Hebrews mentions a city for the first time in verse 10. This emerges as a main theme in the last chapters of Hebrews. In light of God's promises to Abraham and the kind of life he led, what is meant by the city mentioned here?

5. How does this city relate to the topic of faith that has been under discussion?

Faith, it now emerges, is not only the assurance of unseen realities, and the backbone of hope, as in verse 1; it is not only the belief that God exists and rewards those who seek him, as in verse 6; it is also the badge that marks people out as members already of God's true people. Precisely because this faith is also hope, their membership, and their inheriting of God's promises, does not yet appear in public. Faith enables this standing, this "righteousness," to be affirmed in the present time. Hebrews thus agrees more or less exactly with what Paul means by "justification by faith," one of the New Testament's most powerful, encouraging and comforting doctrines.

6. In 11:13-16 the writer says God wasn't ashamed to be called the God of the people mentioned so far in chapter 11. Why might some think God would be ashamed to be called "their God"?

7. Hebrews 11:17-19 recalls the story of Abraham and Isaac (from Genesis 22) and 11:20-22 mentions Isaac and Joseph (from Genesis 27 and 48–50). What further themes about faith, obedience and hope are developed in these stories?

8. *Read Hebrews 11:23-40.* What encouragement do you draw from the example of Moses in verses 23-31?

9. In verses 32-40, there is a long catalog of people who faced terrifying situations, and in many cases were persecuted to within an inch

of their lives if not beyond. Why, if God was at work in the lives of
Gideon, Barak, Samson, and those who were stoned and so on—
why, if God was calling them and was with them, did they have to
go through all that?

10. What does the writer mean by saying in 11:38 that the world didn't
    deserve them?

11. The writer of Hebrews wanted his readers to think through the sort
    of faith their forebears had had, and see how the long purposes of
    God, cherished and believed in the face of impossibilities, dangers
    and even death itself, are finally fulfilled in the events concerning
    Jesus, and the new life they have as a result.

    Considering the heroes of faith in this chapter, what might it mean,
    specifically, to live by faith in God's future world while the society
    all around is living as though the present world is all there is or all
    there will be?

12. Describe one way that you can live by faith in this coming week and
    trust that God will give you strength to live this way.

PRAY

Pray for strength and courage to live by faith as defined and illustrated in Hebrews 11. Pray about the specific ways you could live by faith in the situation you mentioned in the last question. Pray for boldness, strength and trust in that circumstance.

NOTE ON HEBREWS 11:10 AND 16

As mentioned, the writer introduces the image of the city in Hebrews 11:10 and 16, which he develops further in later chapters. The focal point of the promise in chapter 11 is about the land. In Hebrews 12:12 it is the heavenly Jerusalem. In 13:14 it is the future city, contrasted with any city to which one might give allegiance here on earth, and perhaps particularly the earthly Jerusalem itself. What does the writer have in mind?

Jerusalem was of course the holy city, David's ancient capital. But in Jewish writings roughly contemporary with the New Testament, there were pointers to a deeper reality, to the belief that God had established a "true" or heavenly Jerusalem, waiting for the day when heaven and earth would be remade. This is picked up in the great description of the new Jerusalem in Revelation 21–22.

LOOKING TO JESUS

Hebrews 12

If you've ever run in a race, you may find the opening verses of chapter 12 bringing back memories. I remember one cross-country race in which, mile after mile, I was almost alone, with only the few other runners around me for company. But then, when we came round the last turn and into the final few hundred yards of the course, that all changed. Crowds of people were cheering, waving flags, holding signs, clapping and shouting words of encouragement. The noise reached a great roar as we crossed the finishing line itself.

Several aspects of this climactic chapter in Hebrews draw on the same image of the Christian pilgrimage as a long-distance race. Those who have gone before us, from Abel and Abraham right through to the unnamed heroes and heroines noted at the end of chapter 11, haven't simply disappeared. They are there at the finishing line, cheering us on, surrounding us with encouragement and enthusiasm, willing us to do what they did and finish the race in fine style.

OPEN

Think of a competition you were involved in, whether athletic or otherwise. What helped you finish or what caused you to drop out? Explain.

STUDY

1. *Read Hebrews 12.* In verses 1-2, the writer uses athletic imagery. Describe the things he mentions that would help someone run a footrace with efficiency and success.

2. How do each of these parallel or relate to the Christian life?

3. How would verses 2-3 about Jesus' experience and work have served as an encouragement for the early believers in their context?

4. According to verses 4-11, how is discipline from God evidence that we are his beloved children?

The truth of verse 11 is offered so that we can cling to it when things are difficult. There is much sorrow in an ordinary human life; sorrow which was, of course, shared by the Man of Sorrows as he identified completely with us, a point Hebrews has already made forcefully (5:7-10). Again and again, when we find ourselves thwarted or disappointed, opposed or vilified, or even subject to physical abuse and violence, we may in faith be able to hear the gentle and wise voice of the Father, urging us to follow him more closely, to trust him more fully, to love him more deeply.

5. How have you seen this to be true in your own life or the lives of others?

6. Hebrews 12:12-17 recalls the story told in Genesis 25–27 about Isaac's twin sons, Jacob (the younger) and Esau (the older). Esau had been out hunting in the countryside and when he came back home Jacob was cooking a meal. Esau was famished with hunger; Jacob refused to give him food unless he gave him the rights of the firstborn son, in other words, the principal share of the inheritance from their father Isaac. Esau, it seems, happily swore away his birthright in exchange for the food—something he bitterly regretted later. Jacob doesn't exactly come out of the story with his hands clean, but the focus here is on the folly of Esau.

In addition to warning against the immoral or worldly-minded decisions of Esau, verses 12-17 also strongly caution against coasting as a Christian, not seeking spiritual healing, continuing to live in conflict and allowing bitterness to take root in our relationships.

Which of these do you see as most critical to avoid and why?

7. Hebrews 12:18-21 refers to Mount Sinai and Exodus 19 where the people were warned not to touch the mountain and where Moses received the Ten Commandments and the warnings the people were given during that episode. The contrast between Mount Sinai and Mount Zion (or Sion as it is sometimes spelled) in verses 18-24 is not suggesting that holiness doesn't matter any more. How instead are the two mountains contrasted?

8. In verses 18-24 the writer of Hebrews picks up the theme (begun
   in Hebrews 11:10) of the new Jerusalem, the new city we anticipate
   and hope for. While there is still much to look forward to, in what
   senses does the writer suggest here that we have already arrived at
   this heavenly city?

The Old Testament story which began with Abraham, Moses and
Mount Sinai reached its glorious conclusion with the entry into the
Promised Land, the establishment of the monarch and finally the
building of the temple on Mount Zion. Now, Hebrews is saying, take
that story as a whole, and see it as the equivalent of Mount Sinai; it
is the complete story of the old covenant. You need to come into the
Promised Land (Hebrews 3–4); you need to benefit from the ministry of the true high priest (Hebrews 5–7); you need to realize that
you are within the new covenant, where the ultimate sacrifice has
already been made, through which you can approach the very presence of God himself (Hebrews 8–10).

9. How does 12:25-29 bring us back full circle to what the writer began
   with in Hebrews 2:1-4?

10. The central theme that the writer wants to leave with the readers
    before the concluding instructions of chapter 13 is a true picture of
    God and of people in relation to God. What is that picture?

11. Verses 28 tells us our response should be one of gratitude and worship. Why are these proper responses to the kind of God pictured by the writer?

12. How can and should we express these this week?

PRAY

Sit in silence and meditate on the character of God and what he has done in your own life. Speak short sentences of praise as offerings and sacrifices.

NOTE ON HEBREWS 12:15-17

The warning here takes its place alongside those in 6:4-8 and 10:26-31: a warning that to turn back to the ways of the world after tasting at least the fringe benefits of the new life may result in a fixed and unalterable condition of the heart and mind. According to 6:4, it is impossible to restore such people to repentance; this seems to be what 12:17 is saying as well. We should be cautious about suggesting that someone who genuinely wants to repent of their sin and get right with God will ever be refused; but we should be equally cautious about imagining that someone who enjoys Christian fellowship but then plays fast and loose with the consequent moral responsibilities will be able to come back in whenever and however they feel like it. Decisions and actions have consequences.

NOTE ON HEBREWS 12:25-29

The really worrying thing in this passage is that the quaking earth at
Sinai is not replaced with some calm, flat transition to God's new covenant and new world, but with something even more tumultuous—not
only an earthquake but also, so to speak, a heavenquake. As Revelation
21 insists, for there to be new heavens and a new earth, the present
heavens, as well as the present earth, must undergo their own radical
change, almost like a death and new birth.

Hebrews uses a different image for this same transition, but the
end result is the same. Heaven and earth alike must be "shaken"
in such a way that everything transient, temporary, secondary and
second-rate may fall away. Then that which is of the new creation,
based on Jesus himself and his resurrection, will shine out the more
brightly. The new creation will, of course, include all those who belong to the new covenant and, through them, the new world which
God had always promised.

13

THE GOD OF PEACE
BE WITH YOU

Hebrews 13

There is a diary of a clergyman who had been a prisoner of war during 1940 to 1945 in a German prison. I found it a fascinating account of daily life, but frustrating to read, because the Germans would not let people write things in diaries which might be subversive. The result is that quite a few references to current events in the diary were written in a sort of code. The writer would refer obliquely to events or hint at things he knew about the progress of the war, which other prisoners would have picked up at once, but which other readers, without help, could not fathom.

Chapter 13 of Hebrews is not as oblique as all that, but to understand it we need to put ourselves in the situation it refers to. It is quite possible, then, that both writer and readers knew that there was an increasingly tense situation brewing up for followers of Jesus in and around Jerusalem itself. Whether or not this refers to the time when the Jews in Palestine were in revolt against Rome, it is impossible to tell. But certainly that great war (A.D. 66-70), which ended in the destruction of Jerusalem and the temple, would fit very well.

OPEN

As you think about your past, present and future, which of the three weighs on you more than the others or which gives you more cause for hope? Explain.

STUDY

1. *Read Hebrews 13.* At the end of the first section (vv. 1-8) the writer makes a grand statement about Jesus. In looking over the whole letter to the Hebrews, what has it revealed about Jesus in each of these ways—yesterday and today and forever?

2. How does getting our picture right about Jesus in these ways affect the way we engage the practical-life issues raised in 13:1-7?

3. How does 13:1 act as a unifying theme for all the practical matters found in 13:2-7?

4. Look at the topics mentioned in verses 1-7: hospitality, those in prison, marriage, money and Christian leaders. What's a practical way you could follow up in one of these areas this week?

5. What similarities between Jesus and the sacrificial animals of the sin offering does the author highlight in verses 10-14?

6. Once again in 10:14 the writer mentions the future city we have. How does this help us hold lightly to the material goods, position, prestige, accomplishments, family or the other sources of self-worth we get in this world?

7. The writer may have been speaking about the tabernacle in the wilderness during Moses' day rather than the Jerusalem temple to avoid mentioning too directly the central institution of Judaism which Jesus declared to be under God's judgment and whose sacrificial system he replaced. Or it may be that the temple had already been destroyed by the Romans. In either case, the point is that the followers of Jesus should be happy to leave the city and its temple even though their fellow Jews may regard them as traitors.

   With the old sacrificial system defunct, what does 13:15-16 say about the different ways we can bring a continual sacrifice of praise to God?

8. The present mood, particularly in Western society, in which all authority seems suspect, and all power is assumed to corrupt people, gives an extra excuse to people who want to do their own thing rather than submit in any way to someone else. And yet, verses 17-25 suggest there are appropriate structures of responsibility within God's church.

How is the relationship between leaders in the church and the rest of God's people described in these verses?

9. What truths are learned in verses 17-25 about the work of the kingdom?

10. The crowning glory of this final passage is the great blessing in verses 20-21, which is still used regularly in many churches, especially in the Easter season. How do these verses bring Hebrews to a culmination?

11. As you think back over the themes of Hebrews, what truths or challenges have been the most significant for you?

12. How has your life of faith been changed by your journey through this letter?

PRAY

Pray the words of 13:20-21 several times. Pray them as a blessing over family, friends and fellow Christians.

GUIDELINES FOR LEADERS

My grace is sufficient for you.
(2 Corinthians 12:9)

If leading a small group is something new for you, don't worry. These sessions are designed to flow naturally and be led easily. You may even find that the studies seem to lead themselves!

This study guide is flexible. You can use it with a variety of groups—students, professionals, coworkers, friends, neighborhood or church groups. Each study takes forty-five to sixty minutes in a group setting.

You don't need to be an expert on the Bible or a trained teacher to lead a small group. These guides are designed to facilitate a group's discussion, not a leader's presentation. Guiding group members to discover together what the Bible has to say and to listen together for God's guidance will help them remember much more than a lecture would.

There are some important facts to know about group dynamics and encouraging discussion. The suggestions listed below should equip you to effectively and enjoyably fulfill your role as leader.

PREPARING FOR THE STUDY

1. Ask God to help you understand and apply the passage in your own life. Unless this happens, you will not be prepared to lead others. Pray too for the various members of the group. Ask God to open

your hearts to the message of his Word and motivate you to action.

2. Read the introduction to the entire guide to get an overview of the topics that will be explored.

3. As you begin each study, read and reread the assigned Bible passage to familiarize yourself with it. This study guide is based on the For Everyone series on the New Testament (published by SPCK and Westminster John Knox). It will help you and the group if you have on hand a copy of the companion volume from the For Everyone series both for the translation of the passage found there and for further insight into the passage.

4. Carefully work through each question in the study. Spend time in meditation and reflection as you consider how to respond.

5. Write your thoughts and responses in the space provided in the study guide. This will help you to express your understanding of the passage clearly.

6. It may help to have a Bible dictionary handy. Use it to look up any unfamiliar words, names or places. The glossary at the end of each New Testament for Everyone commentary may likewise be helpful for keeping discussion moving.

7. Reflect seriously on how you need to apply the Scripture to your life. Remember that the group members will follow your lead in responding to the studies. They will not go any deeper than you do.

LEADING THE STUDY

1. At the beginning of your first time together, explain that these studies are meant to be discussions, not lectures. Encourage the members of the group to participate. However, do not put pressure on those who may be hesitant to speak—especially during the first few sessions.

2. Be sure that everyone in your group has a study guide. Encourage the group to prepare beforehand for each discussion by reading the

introduction to the guide and by working through the questions in each study.

3. Begin each study on time. Open with prayer, asking God to help the group to understand and apply the passage.

4. Have a group member read aloud the introduction at the beginning of the discussion.

5. Discuss the "Open" question before the Bible passage is read. The "Open" question introduces the theme of the study and helps group members to begin to open up, and can reveal where our thoughts and feelings need to be transformed by Scripture. Reading the passage first will tend to color the honest reactions people would otherwise give—because they are, of course, supposed to think the way the Bible does. Encourage as many members as possible to respond to the "Open" question, and be ready to get the discussion going with your own response.

6. Have a group member read aloud the passage to be studied as indicated in the guide.

7. The study questions are designed to be read aloud just as they are written. You may, however, prefer to express them in your own words.

There may be times when it is appropriate to deviate from the study guide. For example, a question may have already been answered. If so, move on to the next question. Or someone may raise an important question not covered in the guide. Take time to discuss it, but try to keep the group from going off on tangents.

8. Avoid answering your own questions. An eager group quickly becomes passive and silent if members think the leader will do most of the talking. If necessary repeat or rephrase the question until it is clearly understood, or refer to the commentary woven into the guide to clarify the context or meaning.

9. Don't be afraid of silence in response to the discussion questions. People may need time to think about the question before formulating their answers.

10. Don't be content with just one answer. Ask, "What do the rest of you think?" or "Anything else?" until several people have given answers to the question.

11. Try to be affirming whenever possible. Affirm participation. Never reject an answer; if it is clearly off-base, ask, "Which verse led you to that conclusion?" or again, "What do the rest of you think?"

12. Don't expect every answer to be addressed to you, even though this will probably happen at first. As group members become more at ease, they will begin to truly interact with each other. This is one sign of healthy discussion.

13. Don't be afraid of controversy. It can be very stimulating. If you don't resolve an issue completely, don't be frustrated. Explain that the group will move on and God may enlighten all of you in later sessions.

14. Periodically summarize what the group has said about the passage. This helps to draw together the various ideas mentioned and gives continuity to the study. But don't preach.

15. Conclude your time together with the prayer suggestion at the end of the study, adapting it to your group's particular needs as appropriate. Ask for God's help in following through on the applications you've identified.

16. End on time.

Many more suggestions and helps for studying a passage or guiding discussion can be found in *How to Lead a LifeGuide Bible Study* and *The Big Book on Small Groups* (both from InterVarsity Press/USA).

Other InterVarsity Press Resources from N. T. Wright

The Challenge of Jesus
N. T. Wright offers clarity and a full accounting of the facts of the life and teachings of Jesus, revealing how the Son of God was also solidly planted in first-century Palestine. *978-0-8308-2200-3, 202 pages, hardcover*

Resurrection
This 50-minute DVD confronts the most startling claim of Christianity—that Jesus rose from the dead. Shot on location in Israel, Greece and England, N. T. Wright presents the political, historical and theological issues of Jesus' day and today regarding this claim. Wright brings clarity and insight to one of the most profound mysteries in human history. Study guide included. *978-0-8308-3435-8, DVD*

Evil and the Justice of God
N. T. Wright explores all aspects of evil and how it presents itself in society today. Fully grounded in the story of the Old and New Testaments, this presentation is provocative and hopeful; a fascinating analysis of and response to the fundamental question of evil and justice that faces believers. *978-0-8308-3398-6, 176 pages, hardcover*

Evil
Filmed in Israel, South Africa and England, this 50-minute DVD confronts some of the major "evil" issues of our time—from tsunamis to AIDS—and puts them under the biblical spotlight. N. T. Wright says there is a solution to the problem of evil, if only we have the honesty and courage to name it and understand it for what it is. Study guide included. *978-0-8308-3434-1, DVD*

Small Faith—Great God
N. T. Wright reminds us that what matters is not how much faith we have as Who our faith is in. Wright looks at the character of the faith God calls us to. He unfolds how dependence, humility and mystery all have a role to play. But the author doesn't ignore the messiness and difficulties of life, when hard times come and the unexpected knocks us down. He opens to us what faith means in times of trial and even in the face of death. Through it all he reminds us, it's not great faith we need: it is faith in a great God. *978-0-8308-3833-2, 176 pages, hardcover*

Justification: God's Plan and Paul's Vision
In this comprehensive account and defense of the crucial doctrine of justification, Wright also responds to critics who have challenged what has come to be called the New Perspective. Ultimately, he provides a chance for those in the

middle of and on both sides of the debate to interact directly with his views and form their own conclusions. *978-0-8308-3863-9, 279 pages, hardcover*

Colossians and Philemon

In Colossians, Paul presents Christ as "the firstborn over all creation," and appeals to his readers to seek a maturity found only Christ. In Philemon, Paul appeals to a fellow believer to receive a runaway slave in love and forgiveness. In this volume N. T. Wright offers comment on both of these important books. *978-0-8308-4242-1, 199 pages, paperback*